Pop Keyboard 1

INTRODUCTION

Since 1982 Great West Music has been successful in developing new and innovative music education programs that offer excellent curriculum for the teaching of popular music through the use of modern technology. The effectiveness of the programs has been proven through the popularity of the Technics Music Academy (T.M.A.) and continues to grow and provide legitimate, alternative music education today through Tritone Music Systems. These books will teach you how to play popular music on the piano or electronic keyboard through a simple, organized teaching approach. The instructions are easy to understand, and the comprehensive method will ensure you understand all the concepts as you progress from song to song. We are confident that, through the use of today's technology and this proven system, you'll soon be experiencing the joy of making music.

Contents

Compiled and Edited by Merv Mauthe

HAL•LEONARD® CORPORATION
7777 W. BLUEMOUND RD. P.O. BOX 13819 MILWAUKEE, WI 53213

Diagram Of The Keyboard And Notes

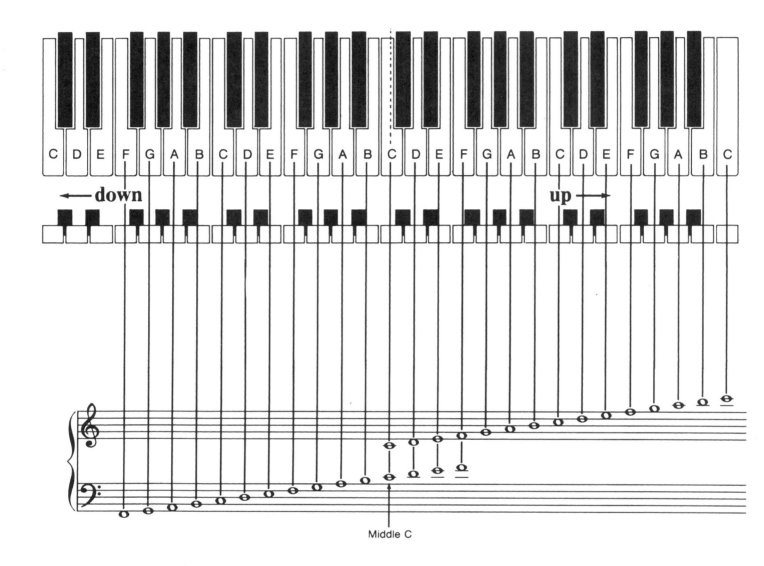

Middle C

A Word About Settings...

The sounds indicated at the beginning of most songs are only basic suggestions. Feel free to adjust them to your instrument, or experiment with your choice of sounds. Certain effects such as sustain, background accompaniments, reverb and volume levels should be added and adjusted at your discretion. Also, rhythms and tempos are simply guidelines which can be altered to whatever style and speed you feel most comfortable with.

Review

Based on music information from the **Introductory Pop Keyboard Course**.

Name the notes and write the number on the corresponding key.

1.
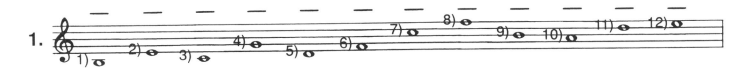

Middle C

2. Fill in any missing beats using ♩, ♩, ♪ or rests.

3. Name the chords and match them with their keyboard position.

_____ Chord •

_____ Chord •

_____ Chord •

• _____

• _____

• _____

4. How many counts?

= _____   = _____   = _____

5. NAME:

mf _____ ||: :|| _____   _____

mp _____   N.C. _____   _____

UNIT 1

Melody

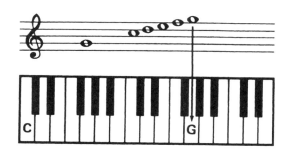

High G is located to the right of F, just above the fifth line.

Prep

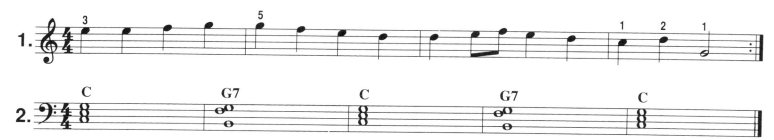

1.

2.
    C   G7   C   G7   C

Theme From The Ninth Symphony

1 Piano   2 Strings   3 Organ

Notes:

---

8 Beat: ♩ = 90 - 100

Prep

1.

2.

Red River Valley

1 🎹 Piano   **2** 🎹 Sax   **3** 🎹 Jazz Organ

Notes:

Swing or 8 beat: ♩ = 120

Melody

High A is located to the right of
G on the first leger line.

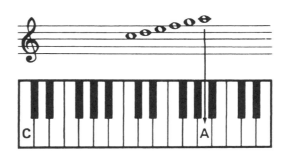

Prep

Oh, Susanna

1 Electric Piano

2 Brass or Clarinet

3 Guitar

Notes:

Accompaniment:

(Ballad Accompaniment)

Melody

High B (above the first leger line) and C (on the second leger line) are located to the right of A.

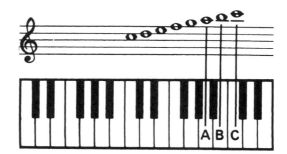

Prep

Reuben And Rachel

1 Electric Piano   2 Synth   3 Flute

Notes:

Swing: ♩ = 180

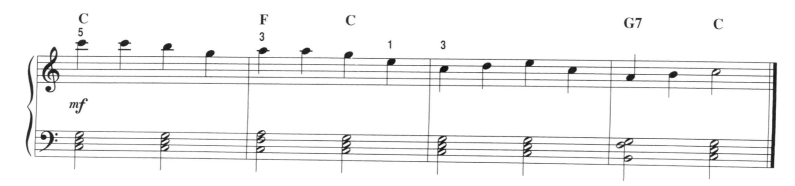

C Major Scale

1. Pay special attention to the fingering of all scales.

2.

3.

Practice the scale above in the following rhythms:

4. Clap or play the rhythms.

Repertoire

Can-Can

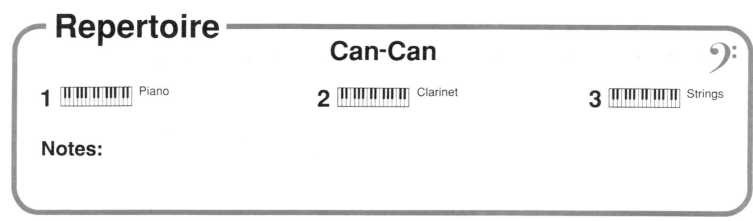

Notes:

Jambalaya
(On The Bayou)

1 Guitar 2 Strings 3 Piano

Notes:

Swing: ♩ = 200
Country: 𝅗𝅥 = 100

Words and Music by
Hank Williams

Accompaniment: 1. 2. 3.

Slurs/Staccato

Notes connected by a slur should be played in a smooth and connected manner (legato)

Staccato (♩) Play the note short and crisp

See page 58 for additional UNIT 1 Repertoire.

Review

Match the following:

1.

- Quarter Note
- Eighth Note
- Dotted Half Note
- Whole Rest
- Dotted Quarter Note
- Half Note
- Two Eighth Notes
- Quarter Rest
- Whole Note
- Half Rest

2. Crossword Puzzle

Down 1.   2.   3.   4.

Across 1.   2.   3.

3. Match the following:

tie •

slur •

f •

N.C. •

<   •

F chord •

‖: :‖ •

>   •

• Repeat

• Crescendo

•

• No chord

• Loud

• Decrescendo

•

UNIT 2

Harmony   Am

The A minor chord (Am)
contains the notes C, E, A.

Find Am as shown.

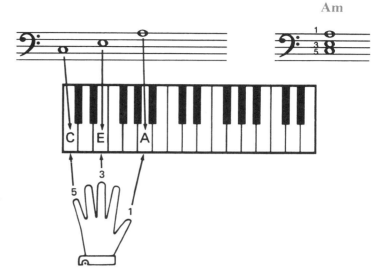

Prep

Stand By Me

Words and Music by Ben E.King,
Jerry Leiber and Mike Stoller

(Repeat to [A])

*Eighth Rest: receives 1/2 beat silence. (page 27)

Accompaniment: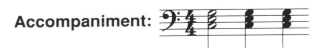

The Bells Of St. Mary's

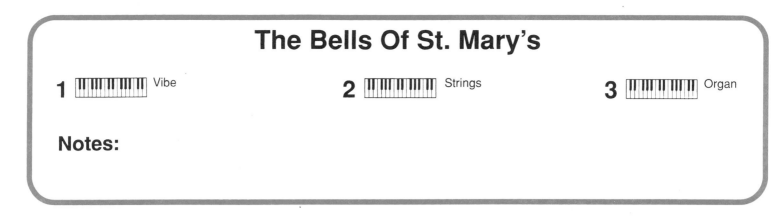

Notes:

Words by Douglas Furber
Music by Emmett Adams

Playing Tip:

The last two measures of "The Bells Of St. Mary's" can be used as an introduction.

Feelings

English Words and Music by Morris Albert
Spanish lyric by Thomas Fundora

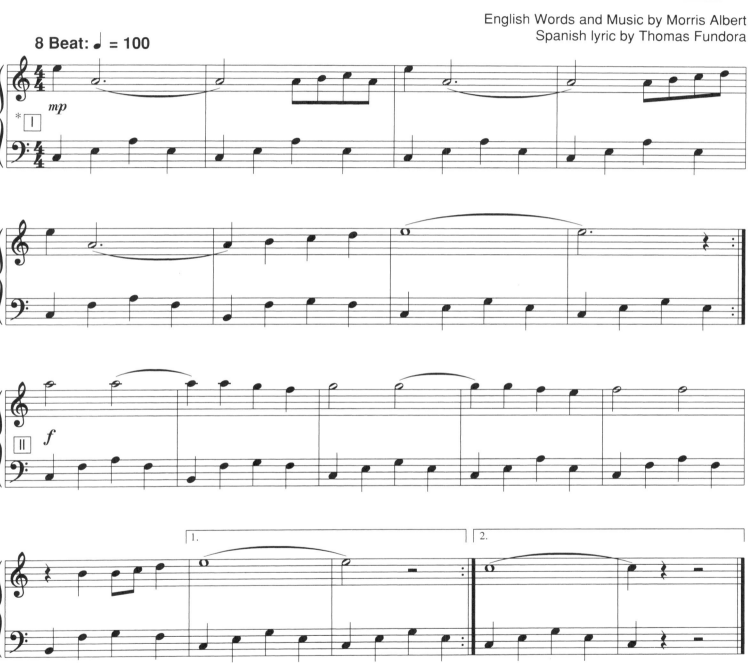

* ☐I ☐II : *Indicates sound change.*

Accompaniment Varitation:

Harmony   Dm

The D minor chord (Dm) contains the notes D, F, A.

Find the Dm chord as shown.

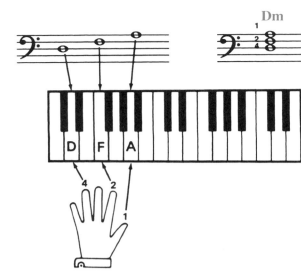

Prep

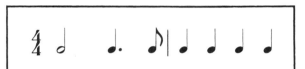

The Drunken Sailor

1 🎹 Harpsichord   **2** 🎹 Strings   **3** 🎹 Synth

Notes:

March: ♩ = 90 or 8 beat: ♩ = 180

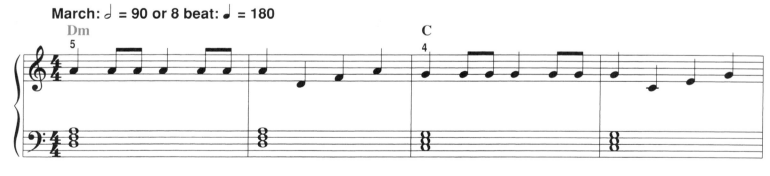

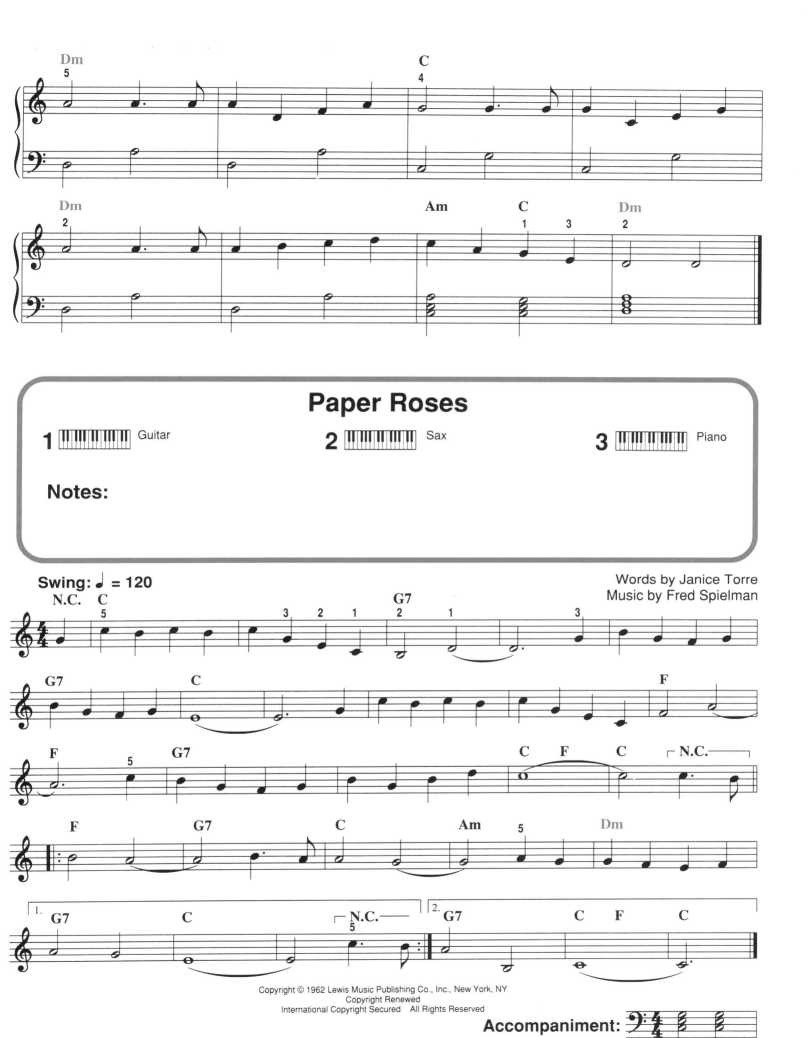

Paper Roses

Words by Janice Torre
Music by Fred Spielman

Harmony   Em

The Em chord contains the
notes B, E, G.

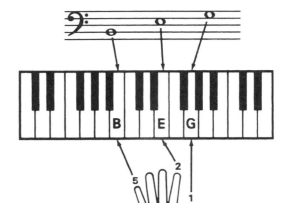

Prep

Snowbird

Notes:

Swing: ♩ = 160

Words and Music by
Gene MacLellan

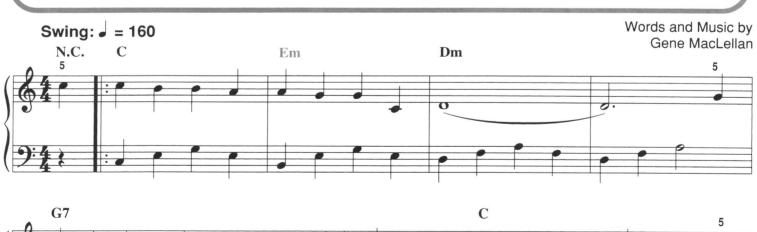

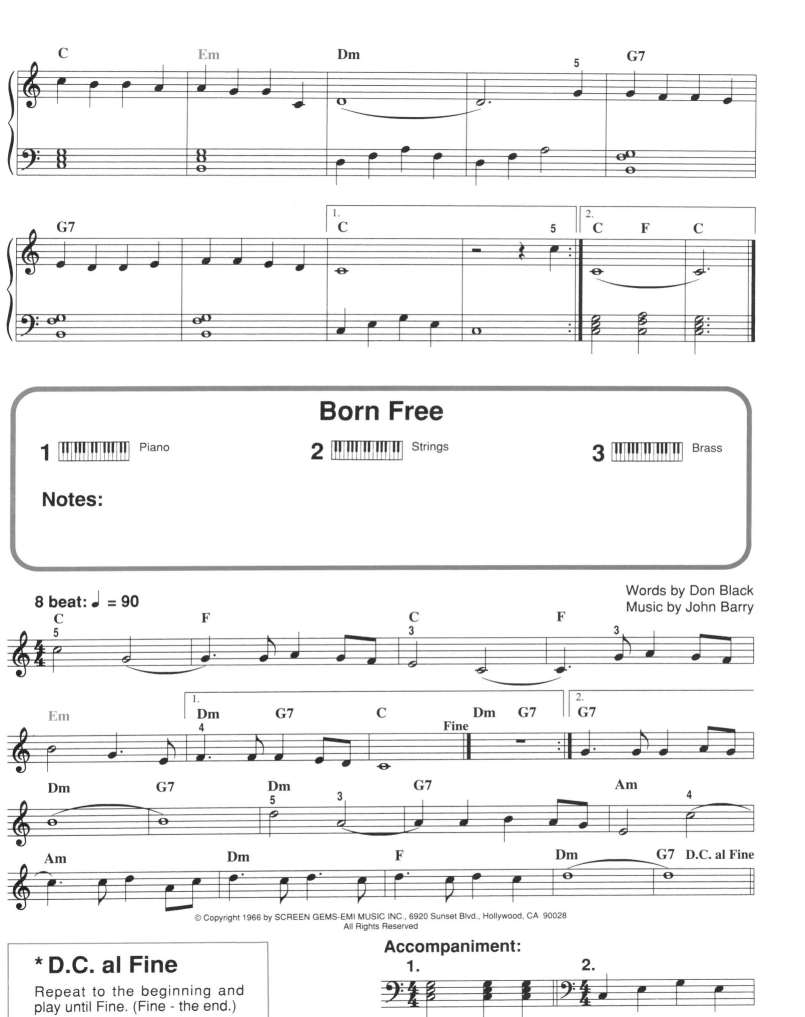

Born Free

1 Piano   2 Strings   3 Brass

Notes:

Words by Don Black
Music by John Barry

8 beat: ♩ = 90

* D.C. al Fine

Repeat to the beginning and play until Fine. (Fine - the end.)

Accompaniment:

1.   2.

EXERCISE

1.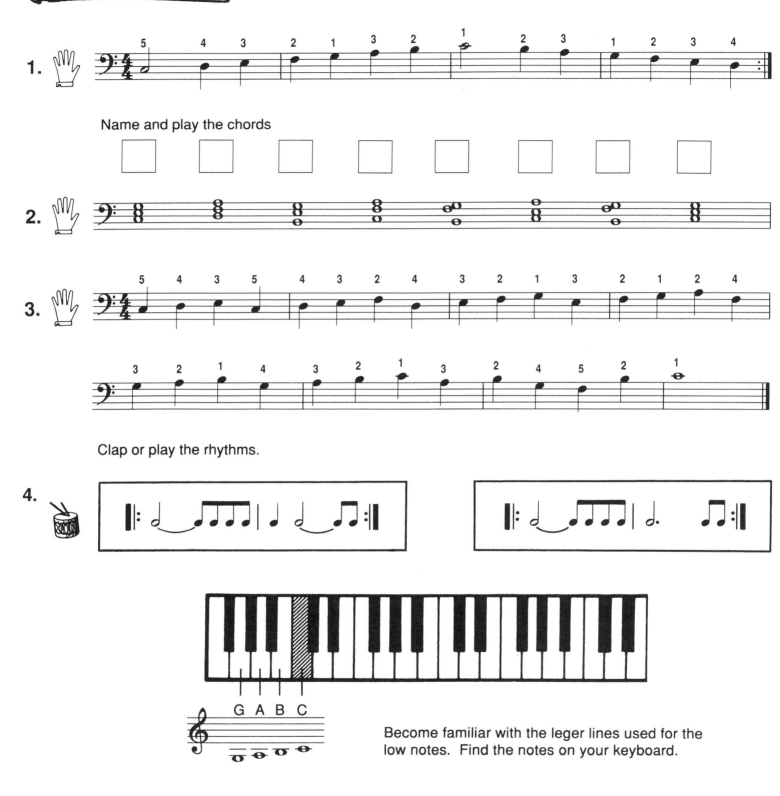

Name and play the chords

☐ ☐ ☐ ☐ ☐ ☐ ☐ ☐

2.

3.

Clap or play the rhythms.

4.

Become familiar with the leger lines used for the low notes. Find the notes on your keyboard.

G A B C

Repertoire

The Rose

1 Piano **2** Electric Piano **3** Strings

Notes:

8 Beat: ♩ = 70

Words and Music by
Amanda McBroom

Octave Sign (8va)

This sign means to play one octave (eight notes) higher than written.

* See page 58 for Additional Unit 2 Repertoire

Review

1. Draw the numbered keys on the staff below.

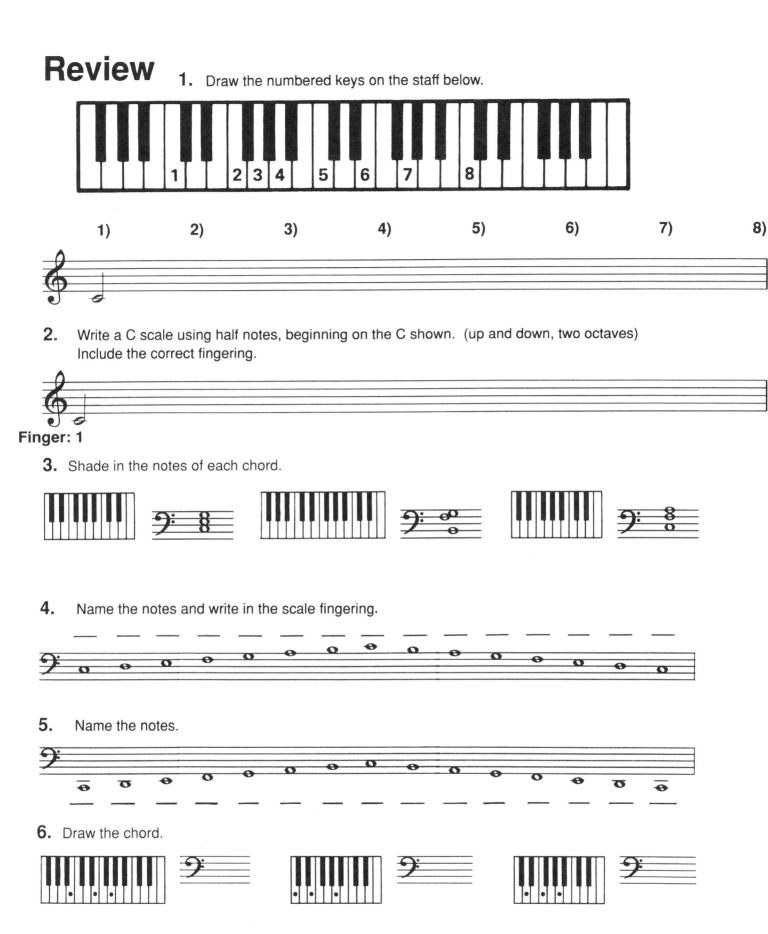

2. Write a C scale using half notes, beginning on the C shown. (up and down, two octaves) Include the correct fingering.

Finger: 1

3. Shade in the notes of each chord.

4. Name the notes and write in the scale fingering.

5. Name the notes.

6. Draw the chord.

7. Draw stems for the following notes:

| Half Note | Dotted Quarter Note | Whole Note | Two Eighth Notes | Quarter Note | Dotted Half Note | Eighth Note | Eighth Note |

UNIT 3

This symbol (#), called a sharp, appears before a note to indicate a raise in pitch. Play the next key to the right, whether that key is black or white.

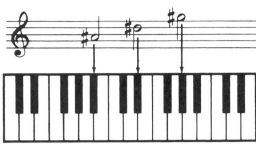

This symbol (♭), called a flat appears before a note to indicate a lowering in pitch. Play the next key to the left, whether that key is black or white.

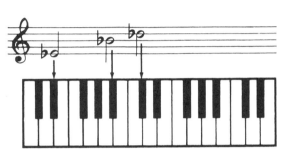

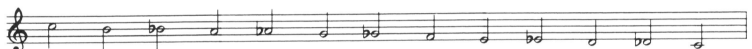

This symbol (♮), called a natural, is used to cancel a sharp or flat. Play the normal white key.

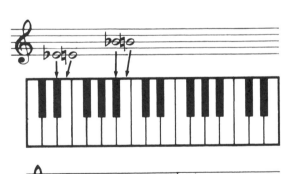

The above symbols are called accidentals, and will affect all identical notes in that measure.
(*Note: The body of these accidentals should be drawn on the same line or in the same space as the note it raises or lowers.)

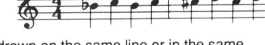

Prep

* See page 32 for the complete version of this song. Also, practice the <u>Chromatic Scale</u> on page 61.

Melody: A New Key

The G scale contains an F#, and is fingered the same as the C scale. Play the scale with the proper fingering.

G Major Scale

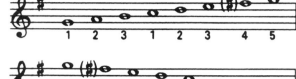

The key of a piece is shown by a key signature. This shows what notes are to be played as sharps or flats throughout the piece.

Key Signature of G major.
All F's are sharp.

Key Signature of C major.
No sharps or flats unless marked.

Prep

Harmony   G   D7

The G major chord contains the notes G, B, D. Find the chord as shown.

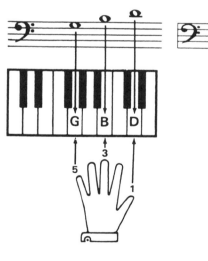

The C major chord and G7 used in the key of G major are in different positions than in previous songs.

Prep

New C Chord Position

The D7 chord contains the notes F#, C, D. Find the chord as shown.

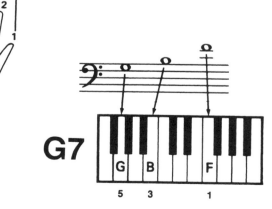

C
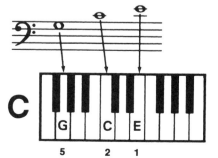

24

Green Green Grass Of Home

1 🎹 Electric Piano   2 🎹 Sax   3 🎹 Guitar

Notes:

Words and Music by
Curly Putman

A **Fermata** or **Pause** tells you to hold the note longer than its normal value (usually twice the actual time value.)

Prep

Tom Dooley

1 ▦ Piano II   2 ▦ Brass   3 ▦ Jazz Organ

Notes:

Words & Music collected, adapted and arranged by
Frank Warner, John A. Lomax & Alan Lomax
From the singing of Frank Proff

8 Beat: ♩ = 126

Key of __ Major

Key of __ Major

Modulation

Sometimes songs change keys part-way through. This is called modulation, and adds color and interest to your playing. In "Tom Dooley" the modulation occurs on line 2, bar 4. The natural sign (♮) which appears there acts as a new key signature and cancels the F♯ in the previous key signature.

Prep

Eighth Rest

The eighth rest corresponds to the eighth note in value, receiving ½ beat silence.

Clap or play the following rhythms.

All I Have To Do Is Dream

1 🎹 Piano   2 🎹 Vibe   3 🎹 Guitar

Notes:

8 beat: ♩ = 100

By Boudleaux Bryant

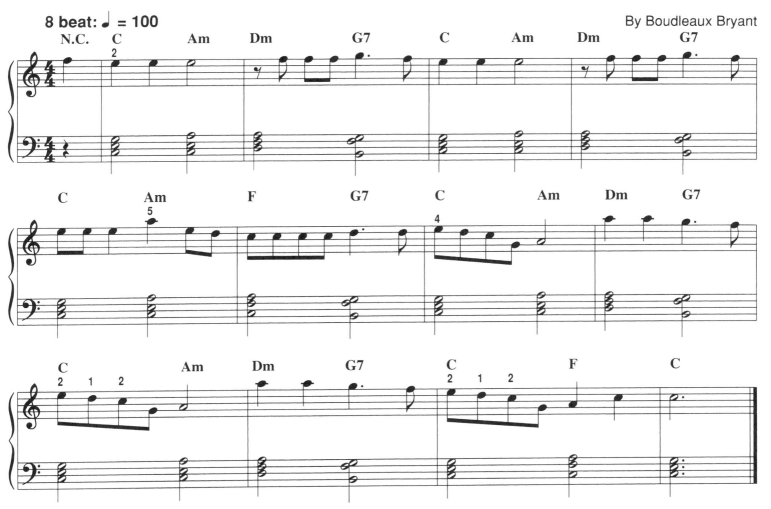

Accompaniment Variation:

New Rhythm

In 3/4 time the Waltz Rhythm is often used to accompany the melody.

Variation

Prep

Skater's Waltz

1 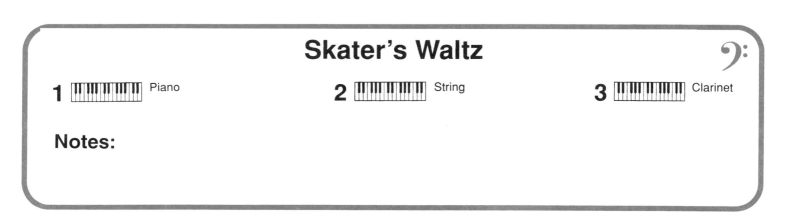 Piano   2 String   3 Clarinet

Notes:

Waltz: ♩ = 140 - 150

Edelweiss
(From "THE SOUND OF MUSIC")

Lyrics by Oscar Hammerstein II
Music by Richard Rodgers

Waltz: ♩ = 120

*Rit. (Ritardando)

Gradually play slower. (Turn off drums at the beginning of the rit. section.)

EXERCISES

G Major Scale

Practice with the waltz rhythm.

Repertoire

I Only Want To Be With You

1  Jazz Guitar   2  Jazz Organ   3 Electric Piano

Notes:

Words and Music by
Mike Hawker & Ivor Raymonde

Alley Cat Song

1 🎹 Piano   **2** 🎹 Synth   **3** 🎹 Jazz Organ

Notes:

Music by
Frank Bjorn

See page 59 for additional Unit 3 Repertoire.

Accompaniment:

1.

2.

Review

1. Draw the accidental in front of the note and match with the correct key.

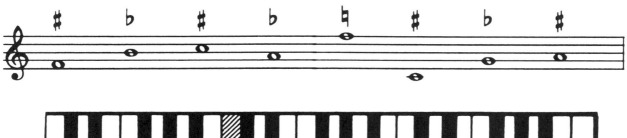

Middle C

2. Write a G scale using quarter notes, beginning on the G shown; (one octave up and down.) Include the correct fingering and any sharps or flats.

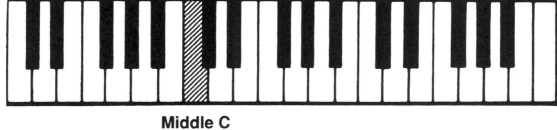

Finger: 1

3. Shade in the notes of each chord.

4. Name the rhythm.

_____   _____

5. Match

Eighth rest •   • 𝄾

Gradually slow down •

D7 chord •   • *8va*

One octave higher •   • *rit.*

Quarter rest •   • 𝄽

G chord •

33

UNIT 4

New Rhythm

The Eighth Note Triplet is a group of three notes that are played in the same time as one quarter note. The number 3 will appear above or below the triplet.

Prep

1.

2.

3.

Amazing Grace

1 🎹 Harpsichord   2 🎹 Brass   3 🎹 Pipe Organ

Notes:

No Rhythm or Waltz: ♩ = 90

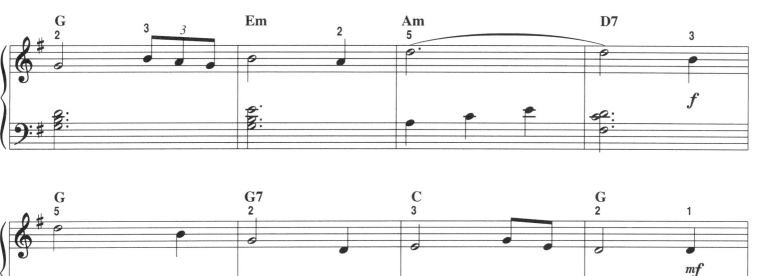

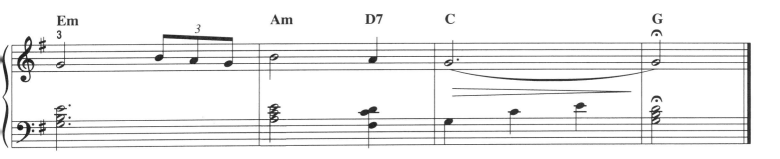

Playing Tip:

For a special "bagpipes" effect play G and D with the left hand for all of the accompaniment. An accordion setting will also make the sound more effective.

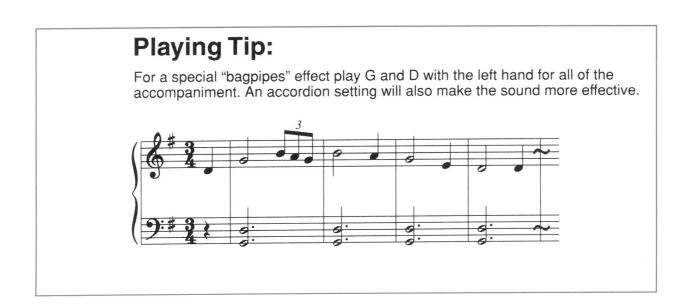

Chariots Of Fire

1 Piano   **2** Flute   **3** String

Notes:

Music by
Vangelis

Ballad: ♩ = 74

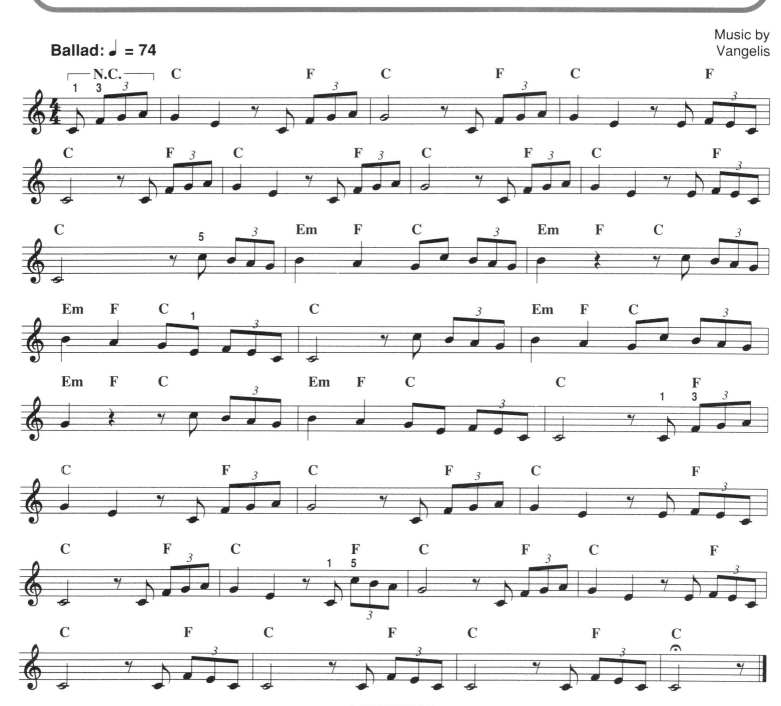

Accompaniment:

Mr. Bojangles

Words and Music by
Jerry Jeff Walker

Waltz: ♩ = 110

New Rhythm

In 4/4 time the Swing rhythm is often used to accompany the melody.

Prep

Little Brown Jug

1 [keyboard] Electric Piano   2 [keyboard] Guitar   3 [keyboard] Clarinet

Notes:

Swing: ♩ = 120

This Land Is Your Land

1 ▦ Piano   2 ▦ Strings   3 ▦ Brass

Notes:

Swing: ♩ = 160

Words and Music by
Woody Guthrie

1. Seventh Chords are really four note chords, however, often a note will be omitted for a smoother accompaniment. Practice the progression below using sevenths in their 4 note version.

4. Practice using the swing rhythm.

Liechtensteiner Polka

1 🎹 Electric Piano   **2** 🎹 Trumpet   **3** 🎹 Accordion or Organ

Notes:

March or Polka: ♩ = 110

Words and Music by Ed Kotscher and R. Lindt

Accompaniment:

Loch Lomond

1 🎹 Piano   2 🎹 Guitar   3 🎹 Sax

Notes:

* See page 60 for additional Unit 4 Repertoire.

Review

1. Name the following chords:

_____ _____ _____ _____ _____ _____ _____ _____

2. Add in bar lines:

3. Fill in the missing notes of the G major scale.

4. Write the chords shown in the diagrams on the staff.

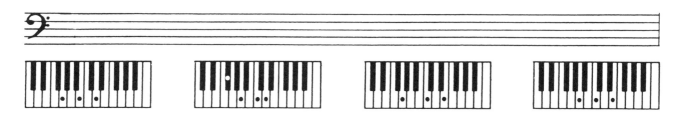

5. Match

♭ •   • Fermata

8va •   • Swing Rhythm

³ ♪♪♪ •   • G7 chord

[bass clef chord] •   • natural

[bass clef chord] •   • triplet

⌢ •   • flat

♮ •   • octave higher

[bass clef chord] •   • D7 chord

UNIT 5

Melody: A New Key

The F scale contains a B♭ note.
The fingering is different from C
and G scales.

F Major Scale

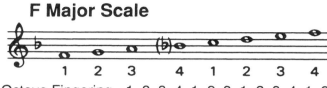

(Two Octave Fingering - 1 ,2 ,3 ,4 ,1 ,2 ,3 ,1 ,2 ,3 ,4 ,1 ,2 ,3 ,4)

**Key Signature
of F major.**

All B's are flat.

Prep

Harmony   B♭   C7

The B♭ chord contains
the notes F, B♭, D.

The C7 chord contains
the notes E, G, B♭, C.
The G is often omitted
from the chord.

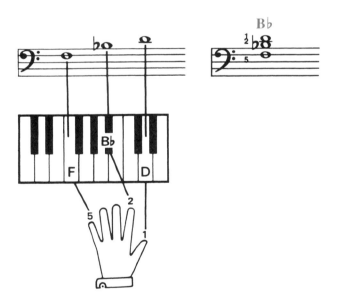

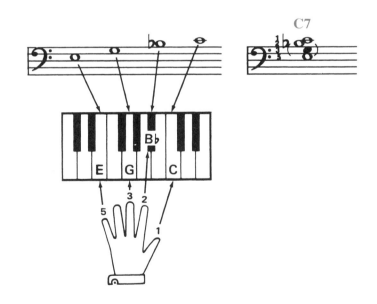

Prep   * (NOTE: New Position for F chord F A C)

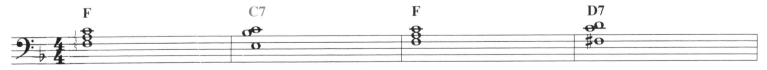

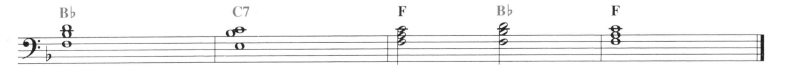

45

Melody In F

1  Piano   **2** String   **3** Sax

Notes:

8 Beat or Ballad: ♩ = 90

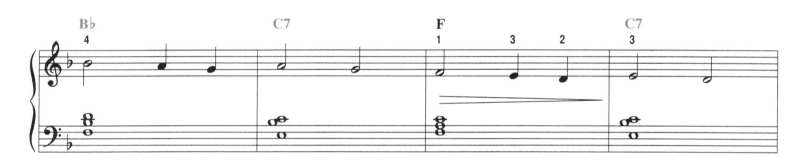

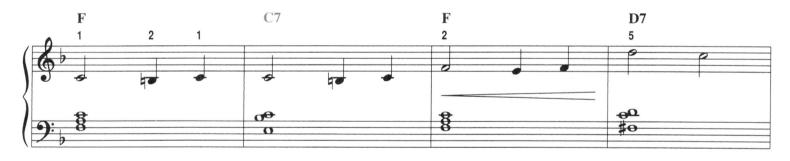

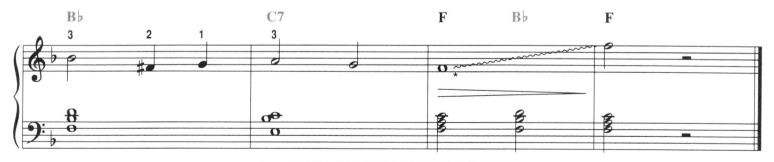

* Glissando   This sign means to slide over the keys, stopping at the note appearing at the end of the glissando.

Beer Barrel Polka

1 🎹 Accordion   2 🎹 Trombone   3 🎹 Piano

Notes:

March: ♩ = 110

by Lew Brown, Wladimir A. Timm,
Jaromir Vejvoda and Vasek Zeman

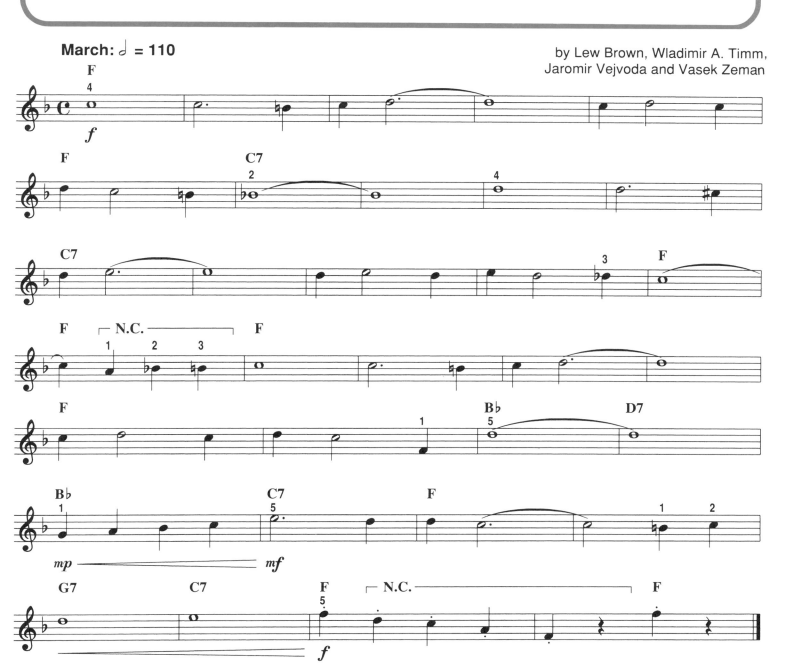

Accompaniment:

C

* This symbol indicates common time, and is another way of showing 4/4.

Walking Bass

This technique is often used to fill in empty sections of a song in order to make the accompaniment more interesting. The left hand moves step-wise, up or down the scale, or plays notes found in the chord.

Bass Boogie

Swing

Prep

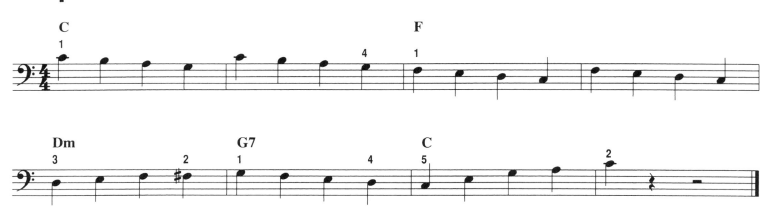

Don't Be Cruel
(To A Heart That's True)

Swing or Shuffle: ♩ = 150 - 160

Words and Music by Otis Blackwell
and Elvis Presley

Star Wars

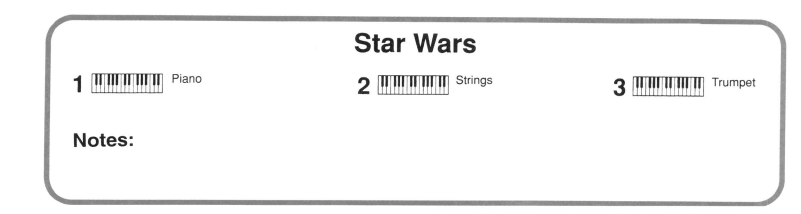

1 Piano **2** Strings **3** Trumpet

Notes:

Disco or Ballad: ♩ = 100

Music by John Williams

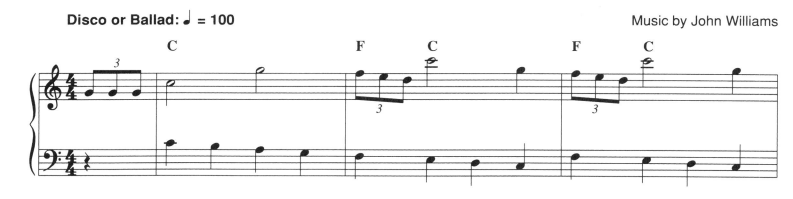

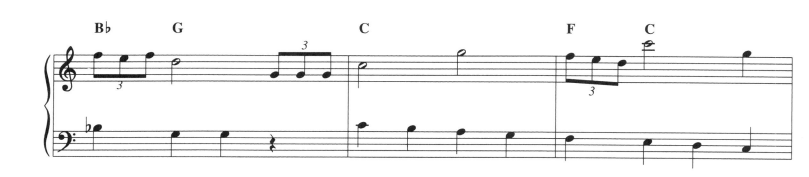

*****Accent** > Special emphasis on a note.

Paloma Blanca

March or Polka: ♩ = 100 - 110

Words and Music by
Hans Bouwens

Alternate Bass

For more variety an alternating note can be used, either before or after the root. The alternate note most often used is the fifth. This technique is often used in swing and waltz accompaniments.

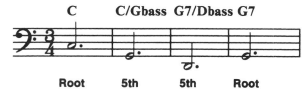

Prep

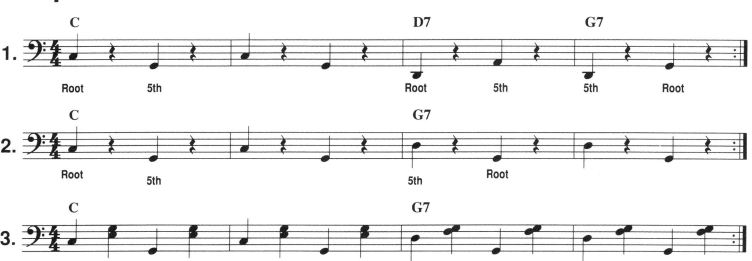

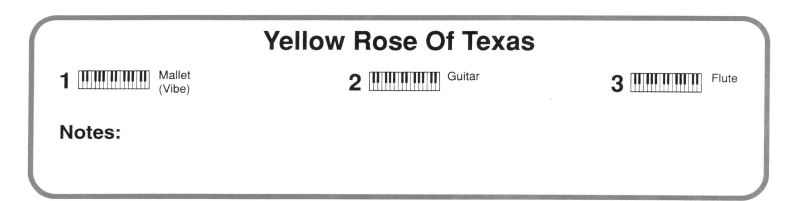

Yellow Rose Of Texas

1 🎹 Mallet (Vibe)   **2** 🎹 Guitar   **3** 🎹 Flute

Notes:

Copyright © 1992 by HAL LEONARD PUBLISHING CORPORATION
International Copyright Secured   All Rights Reserved

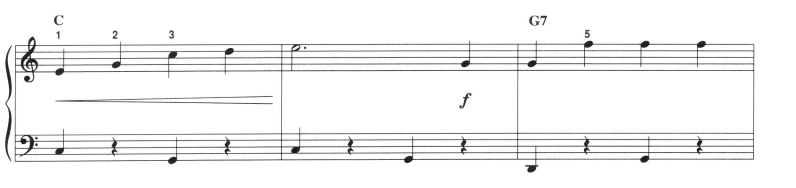

Playing Tip: Go back to other songs you have played and try alternating bass notes.

Scale Review

C major

*(Try scales up and down, two octaves. Fingering: 1 2 3 1 2 3 4 1 2 3 1 2 3 4 5.)
(Down: 5 4 3 2 1 3 2 1 4 3 2 1 3 2 1)

G major

(same fingering as C scale)   F♯   F♯

F major

*(Fingering, Two octaves: 1 2 3 4 1 2 3 1 2 3 4 1 2 3 4)
(Down: 4 3 2 1 4 3 2 1 3 2 1 4 3 2 1)

Broken chords:

Repertoire

Grandfather's Clock

March: ♩ - 90-100

Repertoire

Scarborough Fair

1  2   3

Notes:

Review

1. Transpose the following into the key of G.

2. Draw the alternate for each note.

3. Name the following and give their time value:

Repertoire

Use this section to create your own settings and reinforce each unit.

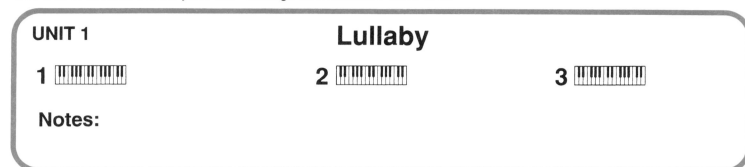

UNIT 1

Lullaby

1 · 2 · 3

Notes:

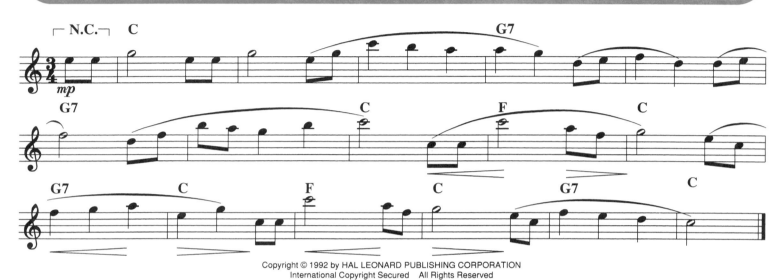

UNIT 2

Camptown Races

1 · 2 · 3

Notes:

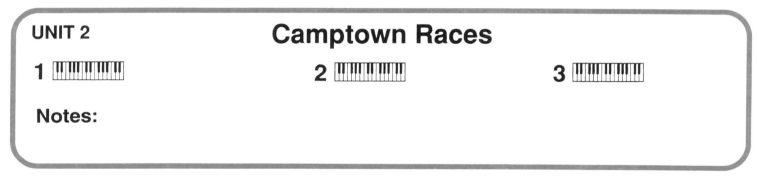

UNIT 3

Lavender's Blue

1 ▦ **2** ▦ **3** ▦

Notes:

UNIT 4

American Patrol

1   **2**   **3**

Notes:

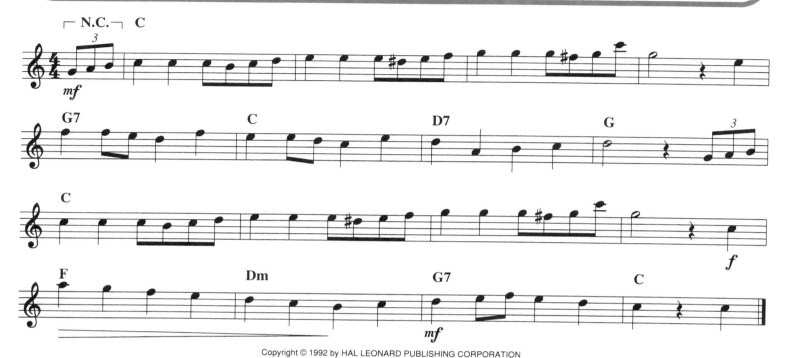

UNIT 5

Julida Polka

1   **2**   **3**

Notes:

Theory Reference
Scale Formation

A scale is made up of a series of half steps and whole steps. A half step is the distance from one key to the nearest key, while a whole step has one key (black or white) in between.

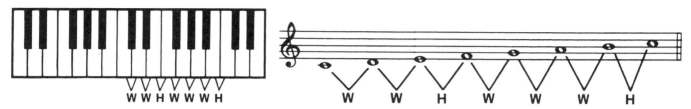

Scales

C major

G major

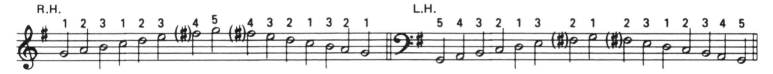

F major

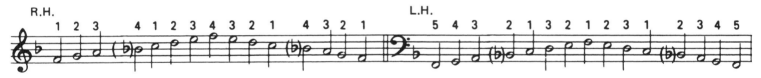

Chromatic Scale (consists of the 12 half steps in an ocatve)

Accompaniment Patterns

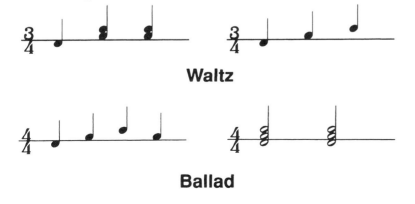

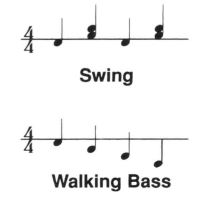

Waltz

Swing

Ballad

Walking Bass

Chord Formation

Chords are formed by combining certain tones of the major scale.
- a Major Chord is made by combining the first (or root), third, and fifth notes of the major scale.
- a Minor Chord is made by combining the root, flatted third and fifth
- a Seventh Chord is made by combining the root, third, fifth and flatted seventh.

e.g. Major Chord   e.g. Minor Chord   e.g. Seventh Chord

Chord Diagrams

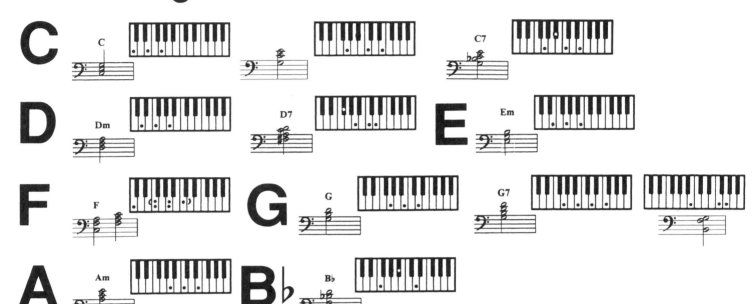

Musical Terms and Symbols

Semitone (or half step) — the distance from one key to the nearest key.

Accidental — a sign placed in front of a note (♯, ♭, or ♮)

♯ — **sharp** (raises a note by a half step)

♭ — **flat** (lowers a note by a half step)

♮ — **natural** (cancels a sharp or flat)

 Key signature — (indicates which black notes are to be played throughout the song)

 Common Time — 4/4 time

8va — play one octave higher than written

Eighth note triplet — (a group of three notes played in the same time as one quarter note.)

Fermata or Pause — (Hold the note longer than its normal value)

Staccato — (play notes short and crisp)

Eighth Rest — ½ beat of silence

 Slur — (play legato or smoothly. Also indicates a musical phrase)

D.C. al Fine — repeat to the beginning and play until Fine.

Modulation — changing keys part-way through the song.

rit. — Ritardando (gradually play slower)

glissando — slide over the keys stopping at the note appearing at the end.

> **Accent** — special emphasis on a note.

Certificate of Merit

This certifies that

_____

has successfully completed

Pop Keyboard Course 1

and is hereby promoted to Pop Keyboard Course 2

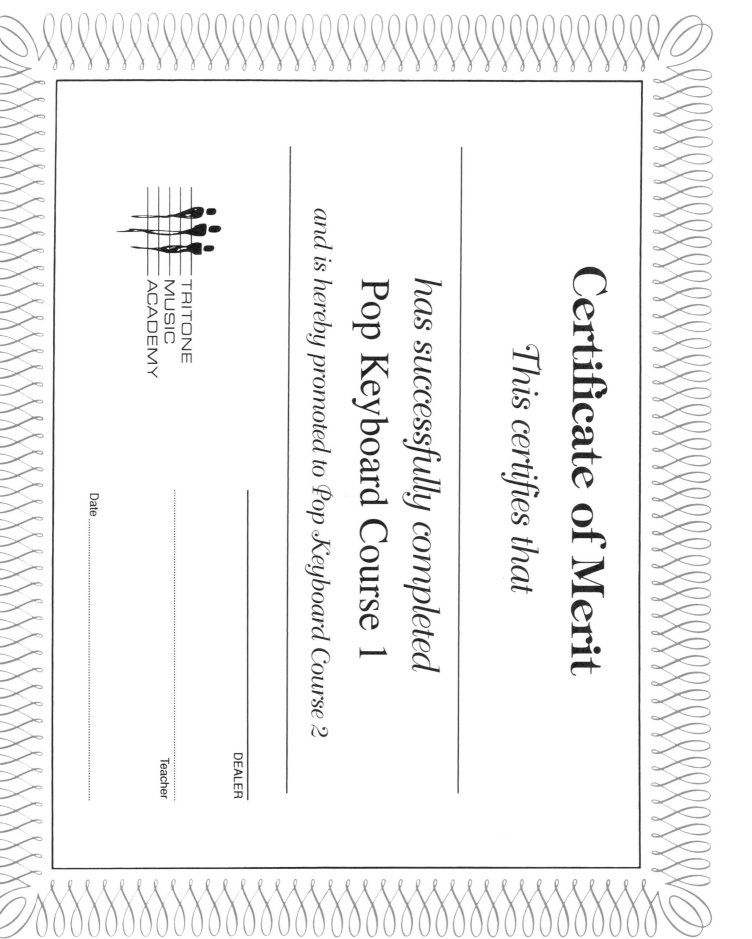

TRITONE
MUSIC
ACADEMY

_____
DEALER

....
Teacher

Date ....